SOUTHERN AND ISLE OF WIGHT RAILWAYS

THE LATE 1940s TO LATE 1960s

Brian Reading and Ian Reading

AMBERLEY

The 1941 introduction of Bulleid's impressive air-smoothed Merchant Navy class, and their 1945 Light Pacific cousins, created a tremendous opportunity for the Southern Railway to make an emotional connection with their passengers, shareholders and business partners. The 110 members of the Light Pacific class were named after West Country locations and after squadrons and heroes of the Battle of Britain. Iconic oval shields were fashioned in vitreous enamel with a cast brass surround. The thirty Merchant Navy class locomotives were named after shipping lines involved in the Battle of the Atlantic or operating from the Southern port of Southampton. Air Chief Marshal Dowding famously led RAF Fighter Command during the Battle of Britain. French Line Compagnie Générale Transatlantique (CGT) operated the SS *Normandie* that, in 1942, caught fire and capsized in New York Harbour while being converted to a troop ship.

First published 2023

Amberley Publishing
The Hill, Stroud
Gloucestershire, GL5 4EP

www.amberley-books.com

ISBN 978 1 3981 0008 4 (print)
ISBN 978 1 3981 0009 1 (ebook)

British Library Cataloguing in Publication Data.
A catalogue record for this book is available from the British Library.

Typesetting by SJmagic DESIGN SERVICES, India.
Printed in the UK.

Introduction

The 1950s and 1960s was an era of post-war renewal and change. In the south of England, a railway generation gap had opened that mirrored the widening generation gap in British society. The Southern Region was simultaneously one of the world's most modern electrified railways and one of the last areas of the UK to operate main line steam locomotives.

Founded by the Railways Act of 1921, the Southern Railway inherited fifty-seven route miles of third-rail electrification. By the late 1930s many more of the lines to the south and east of London had been electrified. On Southern routes to the west of London, until the mid-1960s, steam remained supreme. The characterful creations of Urie, Maunsell and Bulleid could be seen working side by side with charming Victorian survivors and modern BR standard classes.

The Railways Act drove the merger of the London & South Western Railway (LSWR), the London, Brighton & South Coast Railway (LBSCR), the South Eastern & Chatham Railway (SECR) and several smaller companies into the Southern Railway (SR). Robert Urie, the Chief Mechanical Engineer (CME) of the LSWR, and Lawson Billinton, the CME of the LBSCR, retired. In 1923, Richard Maunsell moved forward from the SECR to become the first SR CME.

At the SECR, Maunsell recruited talented engineers from the Great Western and Midland Railways. Under Maunsell's leadership, the SECR blended leading Edwardian locomotive design practice into the class N and many subsequent successful designs. While Maunsell had been a team builder, his successor, Oliver Bulleid, was one of Britain's great railway innovators.

Bulleid's career began in 1901 at the Great Northern Railway (GNR) under Henry Ivatt. In 1908, Bulleid moved to Paris to work for Westinghouse. In the same year, he married Ivatt's youngest daughter Marjorie. By 1919, Bulleid had completed his First World War service with the Royal Engineers and was back with the GNR (and LNER) working with Nigel Gresley. When Maunsell retired in 1937, Bulleid was recruited by the SR as his replacement.

Working with Gresley, Bulleid had the opportunity to contribute to experimental projects including tests in France with poppet valve gear and a Kylchap double blast pipe on the 2-8-2 class P2 *Cock o' the North*. Bulleid arrived at the SR with a flair for innovation and a fully developed sense of self-belief. Challenged to develop motive power for heavy Dover and Folkestone boat trains, he initially proposed 2-8-2 and 4-8-2 designs. Compromising with civil engineers, his concept developed into the 4-6-2 Merchant Navy class, the first Bulleid Pacific.

Bulleid's choice of a 4-6-2 wheel arrangement and three cylinders followed familiar LNER patterns. High tractive effort was delivered by comparatively small 6-foot 2-inch driving wheels and a high boiler pressure of 280 pounds per square inch. High pressure required an all-steel construction that borrowed from United States practice. Thermic syphons were designed into the firebox to improve heat transfer. Aware of the need for footplate ergonomics, a steam powered reverser and firebox doors were added together with ultraviolet gauge lighting for improved night-time visibility. As an innovator, and with the aim of reducing maintenance, Bulleid placed chain-driven Walschaerts valve gear between the frames within an enclosed oil chamber. An air-smoothed boiler casing enabled locomotives to make use of carriage cleaning plants.

Despite wartime austerity, *Channel Packet*, the first of the Merchant Navy class, was introduced in 1941, and from 1945 production of Bulleid's very similar Light Pacific class began. By 1951, the Merchant Navy class numbered thirty and the Light Pacific class numbered 110. Bulleid's all-steel boiler performed well, and early problems with corrosion were solved with careful and consistent water treatment. Where innovation had not been necessary to achieve performance, it led to unreliability. Stretching drive chains affected valve timing, oil baths caught fire, steam reversers jumped into full gear and air-smoothing hampered visibility. Smoke deflector and cab front modifications helped visibility, but running costs remained high. Difficulty using the steam reverser to set valve gear cutoff led to inefficiency. Safety fears led to steam-powered firebox doors being left open for longer than necessary.

In 1953, *Bibby Line* fractured her centre driving wheel crank axle while approaching Crewkerne station at speed. There were mercifully no fatalities, but it was perhaps this incident that catalysed a rebuilding programme that could finally release the potential of Bulleid's almost brilliant designs.

Under the leadership of R. G. Jarvis, all thirty Merchant Navy and sixty members of the Light Pacific class were rebuilt. Air-smoothed casings were removed and conventional Walschaerts valve gear fitted. Rebuilding metamorphosed Bulleid's perhaps idiosyncratic design-concepts into some of Britain's finest steam locomotives.

With a combined fleet of 140, Bulleid's two Pacific classes were visible across the Southern Region. Capable of almost the same power and performance as the larger Merchant Navy class, the Light Pacific fleet were sometimes seen with heavy summer express trains and sometimes on stopping services with just a few coaches.

As the end of the steam era approached, enthusiasts headed south. On lines of the former SR, Bulleid Pacifics were still delivering some of their finest runs. With pictures and recollections, we tour some of the sheds and most characterful routes of the Southern Region. We see the designs of Urie, Maunsell, Bulleid and their predecessors at work between 1948 and 1965. The unique 'Brighton Belle', the world's only electric Pullman train, is captured out of place in 1973.

Pictures are arranged in six sequences:

i) Waterloo, London sheds and the South Western main line to Weymouth
ii) Exeter to Andover Junction with a detour to Bath on the Somerset & Dorset
iii) Winnersh to Newhaven via Redhill and Tunbridge Wells West
iv) Wadebridge to Ilfracombe via Halwill, Bude and Barnstaple
v) Eastleigh Works and the Brighton Belle
vi) Ryde Pier to Ventnor via Havenstreet and Newport

Beginning at Waterloo, the first picture sequence glimpses Nine Elms, Stewarts Lane and Bricklayers Arms sheds before leaving the smoky haze of post-war London to head along the South Western main. After pausing at Fleet, Basingstoke, Winchester and Boscombe, we tour Bournemouth shed before discovering the tranquillity of a summer evening in Meyrick Park. Reversing at Bournemouth West, the southern terminus for the Somerset & Dorset, we arrive at Weymouth to discover the fascinating sight of *Frankton Grange* under repair.

The second sequence begins at Exeter, lingering to tour Exmouth Junction shed before heading east towards Yeovil. At the intersection of the West of England main line and the Somerset & Dorset line, Templecombe reveals motive power from Southern, Western and Midland heritages and an intriguing piloting movement between upper and lower stations. A detour includes scenes of atmospheric Bath Green Park and its wooden shed. Continuing east, pictures taken at Salisbury illustrate Bulleid's Pacific classes in early and late condition, crew change choreography and glimpses of Brunel's former terminus.

Winnersh Halt is the starting point for the third picture sequence, connecting to Redhill on the North Downs line and then on to Tunbridge Wells West, picturesque Oxted, Eridge and south to Polegate Junction on the Cuckoo Line. The tour concludes with a three-cylinder U1 at Eastbourne and a Radial Tank at Newhaven.

The fourth picture tour explores western outposts of the former Southern Railway. At Wadebridge, former GWR 1366 Pannier tanks have arrived from Weymouth. With glimpses of Halwill and Bude, heading north to Barnstaple reveals a shed without a roof. Behind Ilfracombe turntable, a curved rock wall provides a backdrop for a Light Pacific and a tale of a footplate ride by Mr Bulleid.

A tour beside the shed at Eastleigh provides an opportunity to explore the heritage of the Southern Railway. The fifth picture sequence includes designs from the SECR, LSWR and LBSCR, and concludes with two of Bulleid's enigmatic masterpieces. A picture of the Brighton Belle, out of place at Mistley, acknowledges the Southern Railway's role as a pioneer of electrification.

The final set of pictures begins at Ryde Pier Head. Via Havenstreet and Newport, the sequence continues to the south coast of the Isle of Wight and Ventnor, the stunning backdrop for a picture of *Shorwell*, who with her O2 classmates had made the island their own.

We hope the range of illustrations will bring back memories for those who lived through the steam era and inspire the imagination and curiosity of those who enjoy preserved railways today.

Finally, we would like to thank railway historian Richard Adderson for his generous assistance, Catriona and Kathleen for their help with research and proofing, and the Amberley team for their support and encouragement.

Sequence of routes and picture locations

1 Waterloo, London sheds and the South Western main line to Weymouth

2 Exeter to Andover Junction with a detour to Bath on the Somerset & Dorset

3 Winnersh to Newhaven via Redhill and Tunbridge Wells West

4 Wadebridge to Ilfracombe via Halwill, Bude and Barnstaple

5 Eastleigh Works and the Brighton Belle

6 Ryde Pier to Ventnor via Havenstreet and Newport

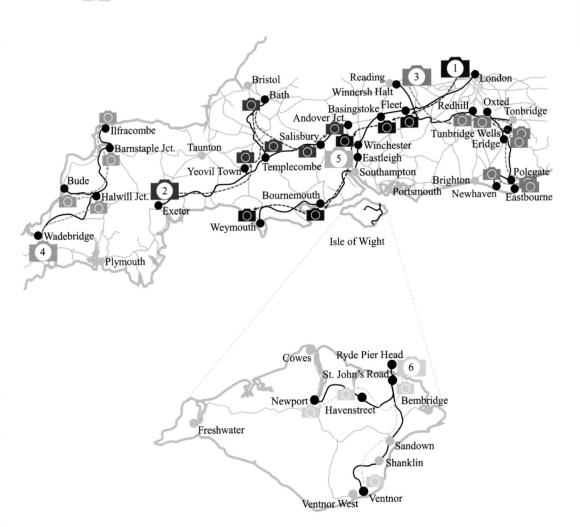

London Waterloo *c.* 1962, 'Ocean Liner Express' passengers gaze towards the camera as they wait to depart for Southampton Docks. Rebuilt Merchant Navy class No. 35006 *Peninsular & Oriental S. N. Co.* prepares to head west. Withdrawn in 1964, No. 35006 was rescued from Woodham Brothers scrapyard in 1983. Restored and steaming since 2015, she can be seen today on the Gloucestershire Warwickshire Railway.

Rebuilt Light Pacific class No. 34025 *Whimple* simmers at London Waterloo *c.* 1962. Bulleid's West Country and Battle of Britain Light Pacific class were competent locomotives, sharing all but the hardest turns with their heavier and more powerful Merchant Navy cousins.

Safety valves roaring, rebuilt Merchant Navy class No. 35028 *Clan Line* is eager to depart with the 'Atlantic Coast Express', the Southern Region's premier daily train to the South West. Class M7 0-4-4T No. 30052 is busy working empty stock. The recently completed Shell Centre towers over Waterloo station. Pictured *c.* 1962, it was the UK's tallest office building.

Built in 1948, No. 35028 *Clan Line* was one of the last members of the Merchant Navy class of thirty. The Southern Region had no water troughs so Bulleid's tenders were large. Pictured *c.* 1962, at London Waterloo, her 6,000-gallon tender had the largest capacity of any UK design. *Clan Line* is preserved, based at Stewarts Lane depot, and often seen hauling main line steam specials.

Above: Despite her roaring fire and deafening safety valves, *Bibby Line* tiptoes out of Waterloo. Improved by rebuilding, Bulleid's 4-6-2 designs continued to have poor adhesion. Fighting for grip, the Pacific's driver deploys sand as the train pulls away. In 1953, No. 35020 *Bibby Line* infamously fractured her centre driving wheel crank axle while approaching Crewkerne station at speed. No one was injured but flying debris caused the station canopy to collapse.

Right: Pictured in 1962, rebuilt Merchant Navy class No. 35005 *Canadian Pacific* prepares to leave Waterloo with an express for Bournemouth and Weymouth. From 1948 to 1951, No. 35005 was experimentally fitted with a Berkeley mechanical stoker that increased coal consumption but sadly not performance. The 1956 to 1960 rebuild of the Merchant Navy class transformed their appearance and potential. *Canadian Pacific* was one of several members of her class to be recorded at speeds over 105 mph.

Rebuilt Merchant Navy class No. 35004 *Cunard White Star* with safety valves lifting pauses at Waterloo *c.* 1962. The potential of Bulleid's innovative but unreliable Merchant Navy design was finally realised by Jarvis' rebuilding programme. Three sets of Walschaerts valve gear replaced Bulleid's troublesome chain-driven original. Boxy air smoothing was removed, and a tubular smokebox added to an already excellent boiler.

Former Great Western Railway Pannier Tanks were used during the early 1960s at Waterloo for empty stock working. Pictured *c.* 1962, Collett 5700 class No. 4616 rolls into the station past the patiently waiting *Cunard White Star*. Opened in 1936, Waterloo signal box, with its iconic concrete architecture, was the largest on the Southern Region. The original Westinghouse power lever frame remained in service until a 1984 signalling upgrade. Sadly, the building was closed in 1990 and demolished as part of the Eurostar project.

As *Cunard White Star* waits for the road to Nine Elms depot, class M7 No. 30039 prepares for her next empty stock duty. Drummond's 0-4-4T class were built for the London & South Western Railway (LSWR) in batches from 1879 to 1925, with some fitted for push-pull working. Pictured *c.* 1962, No. 30039 was withdrawn months later in 1963 after nearly sixty-five years of service.

Merchant Navy class No. 35004 *Cunard White Star* in the distance teams up with her Light Pacific cousin No. 34010 *Sidmouth*. Reversing as a pair to Nine Elms depot reduces line occupancy on this busy day at Waterloo *c.* 1962. Visually and mechanically similar, the Light Pacific has a slightly smaller boiler, shorter frames and a smaller tender. *Sidmouth* is preserved and currently undergoing restoration.

Pictured *c.* 1962, rebuilt Light Pacific class No. 34040 *Crewkerne* reverses out of Waterloo towards Nine Elms depot with empty stock in tow. Forty-eight members of Bulleid's Light Pacific class were named after West Country locations, while most of the remaining sixty-two were named in honour of RAF squadrons, airfields, aircraft and heroes of the Battle of Britain.

Waterloo is a busy terminus and this was certainly true in this 1962 image. Rebuilt Light Pacific No. 34077 *603 Squadron* sets off with a West of England working, while a BR Standard Class 3 2-6-2T brings in empty stock for the next working to Weymouth. Coaches have the Southern Region's characteristically green livery.

Rebuilt Light Pacific class No. 34109 *Sir Trafford Leigh-Mallory* reverses out of Waterloo towards Nine Elms depot, *c.* 1962. Just sixty members of the Light Pacific class were rebuilt. No. 34109, the penultimate class member was built in 1950, rebuilt in 1961 and withdrawn shortly after in 1964. No. 34109 was named in honour of Air Chief Marshal Sir Trafford Leigh-Mallory, KCB, DSO & Bar, commander of Second World War Fighter Groups defending the approach to London.

Reversing out of Waterloo with empty stock under clouds of smoke, BR Standard Class 5 No. 73116 *Iseult* makes a moody silhouette. In 1962, London air was thick, with ten times the current level of suspended particulate matter. *Iseult* was one of twenty class members to receive names from withdrawn LSWR class N15 King Arthur locomotives. Princess Iseult of Ireland was besotted by Sir Tristan in the legendary tales of King Arthur.

Conceived by Robert Urie for the LSWR in 1914, the H15 was an early 4-6-0 mixed-traffic design. Built with outside cylinders and Walschaerts valve gear to ease maintenance, and a large eight-wheel tender for range, the H15 class were used for fast freight and occasional express passenger duties. Pictured beside Nine Elms shed in the mid-1950s, No. 30523 was one of a batch built under Maunsell at Eastleigh in 1924. Nine Elms depot was redeveloped in 1971 and is now the site of New Covent Garden, the UK's largest wholesale fruit, vegetable and flower market.

With over 120 allocated locomotives and 700 staff, Stewarts Lane was a busy depot. Pictured *c.* 1956, former London Brighton & South Coast Railway (LBSCR) 0-6-0T class E2 No. 32102 stands in the foreground. Right of frame, former South Eastern & Chatham Railway (SECR) 0-4-4T class H No. 31266 dates from 1905. The shiny tender on the left belongs to BR Standard Class 5 No. 73082 *Camelot*, introduced just months earlier in 1955 and inheriting her name from King Arthur class No. 30742. Rescued from scrap, No. 73082 *Camelot* is preserved on the Bluebell Railway.

While much of Stewarts Lane depot can still be seen today, one mile northeast, in the shadow of Battersea Power Station, Nine Elms has been levelled and redeveloped. Three miles east, Bricklayers Arms depot has become a trading and logistics centre, with just a few traces of railway architecture still visible. Pictured in the mid-1950s class D1 No. 31739 simmers at Bricklayers Arms. Class D1 was a large boiler and superheated 1913 Maunsell rebuild of a 1901 SECR Wainwright design.

Class Q1 No. 33002 pictured at Bricklayers Arms in the mid-1950s. Unmistakably a Bulleid concept, with Firth Brown wheels and utilitarian appearance, the Q1 was a successful wartime austerity design. Introduced in 1942, the class retain the honour of being Europe's most powerful 0-6-0 steam locomotives.

Left: A mid-1950s view inside Bricklayers Arms shed with class N No. 31872 undergoing maintenance. Rods, pony truck and piston-valve covers have been removed for inspection. Introduced in 1917, Maunsell's two-cylinder class N was inspired by Churchward's 4300 class 2-6-0 and formed a foundation for his later three-cylinder class N1.

Below: Looking northeast towards Fleet, near the site of the original 1847 Fleet Pond station, on the South Western main line. Class T9 4-4-0 gallops along the Down slow line towards Basingstoke. Introduced by Drummond for the LSWR in 1899 and capable of 85 mph, they were affectionately known as 'Greyhounds'. From 1922, Urie improved the class with superheaters. The locomotive pictured is an early class member with splashers shaped around the coupling rods. Pictured in 1948, soon after nationalisation, she has not yet been fitted with a smokebox number plate.

Basingstoke, *c.* 1949, Kodak Box Brownie shaking a little with the excitement of the moment. Merchant Navy class No. 35019 *French Line CGT* in air-smoothed condition takes a deep breath and heads for Waterloo. She carries BR numbers but still wears Southern Railway (SR) livery and tender lettering. The Merchant Navy class was rebuilt from 1956 to 1960 to remove their air-smoothed casing, chain driven valve gear and other less successful Bulleid features. The pneumatic signal gantry at the east end of Basingstoke was in service from 1907 to 1966. On other pages, *French Line CGT* is pictured in later condition at Weymouth and Salisbury.

Pictured *c.* 1949 beside Basingstoke shed, King Arthur class N15 No. 30451 *Sir Lamorak* has Southern lettering on her tender and BR numbering. As a Maunsell continuation of Urie's earlier N15 design, No. 30451 was one of a batch built at Eastleigh in 1925. Maunsell made steam pipe, valve and cylinder refinements. In common with others in her batch, No. 30451 was equipped with a Drummond eight-wheel inside-frame watercart tender from earlier G14 and P14 classes.

Spotlessly clean, class N15 King Arthur No. 30741 *Joyous Gard* rests near Basingstoke shed, *c.* 1949. Fitted with a BR number plate, she still proudly shows off her post-war Southern Railway green livery. No. 30741 was one of a batch built by the LSWR at Eastleigh in 1919, under Urie, with eight-wheel tenders. She was one of five class members upgraded by Bulleid with a wide chimney and Lemaître exhaust as part of a programme that was cut short by the Second World War. The five-nozzle blastpipe was named after Belgian engineer Maurice Lemaître. Sadly No. 30741 was withdrawn in 1956.

Class S15 No. 30506 turns at Basingstoke *c.* 1949. Urie designed the S15 for the LSWR as a freight version of the N15. While they do share some components, the S15 has 5-foot 7-inch driving wheels compared with the larger 6-foot 7-inch wheels used on the N15 King Arthur class. Dating from 1920, No. 30506 was one of the first batch constructed. She was withdrawn in 1964, preserved and operates on the Mid Hants Railway.

Class U No. 31633 beside Basingstoke shed *c.* 1949. Steam leaking past the regulator escapes from open cylinder cocks. It was important to leave locomotives in mid-gear with the tender handbrake firmly applied and cylinder cocks open. Maunsell's successful 1928 U class of fifty locomotives was an evolutionary improvement of his earlier N class design. Twenty U class locomotives were rebuilt from the unsuccessful 2-6-4T K class. Large cab front windows and higher running plates identify No. 31633 as a new build locomotive. She was one of the last batch of ten built in 1931.

Basingstoke Shed in the late 1950s. Brutally functional Q1 No. 33023 stands in contrast to the flowing lines of a former GWR Hall class 4-6-0. Wartime austerity and Bulleid's exuberant self-confidence shaped his 1942 Q1 class of forty locomotives. Bulleid's powerful 0-6-0 freight class shared many concepts with his larger designs.

Winchester City *c.* 1956, class S15 No. 30511 pauses with a breakdown train. The Eastleigh-based 36-ton steam crane was built in 1918 for the LSWR by Ransomes & Rapier of Ipswich and remained in service until 1965. In contrast with the S15 pictured at Basingstoke, No. 30511 is paired with an outside frame bogie tender.

Push-pull fitted class M7 No. 30379 pauses at Winchester City *c.* 1956. The Westinghouse pump mounted on the smokebox pressurised the air reservoir visible under the front buffer beam. A pneumatic actuator on the front of the side tank was connected to a lever in the cab that could move the regulator. An auxiliary reservoir mounted on top of the side tank held air to close the regulator if the system failed. In push mode, the driver remote-controlled the regulator, and made use of an air whistle and vacuum brakes. The fireman controlled the reverser from the locomotive cab.

Former GWR locomotives were regularly seen on Southern Region routes. Pictured *c.* 1956, 4900 Hall class No. 5945 *Leckhampton Hall* rolls into Winchester City on her way to Southampton.

King Arthur class N15 No. 30748 *Vivien* rumbles south through Winchester City with a mixed freight train. *Vivien* is named after the Lady of the Lake who, in many myths, provided King Arthur with the sword Excalibur. Pictured *c.* 1956, No. 30748 was introduced in 1922 and sadly withdrawn in 1957.

Slowing, just one mile before Bournemouth, rebuilt Light Pacific No. 34010 *Sidmouth* rolls into Boscombe from the east. Pictured in 1963, it's hard to imagine that underneath the soot and grime, No. 34010 wears BR lined green livery. *Sidmouth* was built to Bulleid's air-smoothed design in 1945, rebuilt in 1959 and withdrawn in 1965. Mercifully, she was rescued from Barry scrapyard in 1982. At the time of writing, optimism remains that one day she will steam again.

Boscombe, 1963, No. 35011 *General Steam Navigation* accelerates with a train from Bournemouth to Waterloo. With iconic circular nameplates, the Merchant Navy class honoured shipping lines involved in the Battle of the Atlantic or operating from the Southern port of Southampton. No. 35011 was built in 1944, rebuilt in 1959 and withdrawn in 1966 with 1,069,128 miles on her clock. Rescued from scrap, she is currently being restored on the Swindon and Cricklade Railway.

Pictured in 1963, Merchant Navy class No. 35028 *Clan Line* runs eastbound through Boscombe with a train for Waterloo. On her cab side, just a hint of green shows through an otherwise even matt black coat of soot. Maintained today in gleaming condition, *Clan Line* is preserved, based at Stewarts Lane, and regularly stretches her legs with main line steam specials.

BR Standard Class 4 4-6-0 No. 75066 runs east through Boscombe. Designed by Riddles and built at Swindon in 1955, No. 75066 was one of fifteen class members fitted with a large 4,725-gallon type BR1B tender. Without water troughs, the Southern Region was served best by locomotives with large tenders. Sadly, Boscombe station was closed in 1965 and No. 75066 was scrapped at Cashmore's in 1966. Few traces of either remain today.

Bournemouth Central, looking eastwards, summer 1963. In the shade beside the long Down platform, former GWR Modified Hall class No. 6979 *Helperly Hall* prepares to depart. Rebuilt Merchant Navy class No. 35025 *Brocklebank Line* glows in the sun as she runs in from the west with a train for Waterloo. *Brocklebank Line* was withdrawn in 1964, rescued from Barry scrapyard in 1986 and stored for many years. Now in the hands of Southern Locomotives Ltd, optimism is growing that restoration might soon be possible.

Rebuilt Light Pacific class No. 34029 *Lundy* heads under Holdenhurst Road bridge at the eastern end of Bournemouth station. With safety valves enthusiastically lifting, she's eager for the 108-mile run to Waterloo. Built at Brighton in 1946, she was rebuilt in 1958. Pictured in 1963, she was sadly withdrawn in 1964. The original 1870 to 1885 Bournemouth East station was on the other side of Holdenhurst Road bridge.

BR Standard Class 4 2-6-0 No. 76027 departs to the west. Designed by William Jacob and opened in 1885 as the new Bournemouth East, much of the station pictured in 1963 remains today. Renamed Bournemouth Central in 1899, and Bournemouth in 1967, the station was badly damaged by the Great Storm of 1987. Refurbishment in year 2000 restored much of Bournemouth's original character. The long Down platform added in 1928 could accommodate two twelve-coach trains. Its track formation helped divide trains, with separate portions running on to Weymouth and Bournemouth West.

Bournemouth Central's long platform provided a grandstand view of the station and depot. Rebuilt Light Pacific class No. 34082 *615 Squadron* in the foreground stands in contrast to her un-rebuilt classmate. Standing beside the shed in the distance, No. 34038 *Lynton* still has Bulleid's air-smoothed body and chain-driven valve gear. Just sixty members of the Light Pacific class were rebuilt by Jarvis. Pictured in 1963, *Lynton* was one of fifty to spend their entire lives in air-smoothed condition.

Clattering through crossovers to announce her arrival, BR Standard Class 5 No. 73020 rolls in from the west. Pictured in 1967, the last year of her life, she is sadly showing signs of neglect. Much of Bournemouth Central is still recognisable. This vantage point today is in the shadow of the A338 Wessex way that runs on a flyover across the station.

The driver of class M7 No. 30127 ponders with his newspaper, perhaps catching up on the Great Train Robbery or the Profumo affair, two of 1963's headlines. Passengers on the Down platform may not have realised that above them, a signalman was hard at work. Bournemouth Central, a Southern Railway type 11C signal box, was opened in 1928 with a sixty-lever Westinghouse frame. Remaining in service until 2003, its now a listed building.

A view of the fireman's side of class M7 No. 30127 performing her station pilot shunting duties. With slide-valve inside cylinders and Stephenson valve gear, the M7, Drummond's first design for the LSWR, was introduced in 1897. Built at Eastleigh in 1911 and pictured in 1963, No. 30127 is in the last of her fifty-two years of service.

Ivatt's 1946 Class 2 contrasts with Drummond's Victorian M7 0-4-4T design. With outside cylinders, piston valves, Walschaerts valve gear, taper boiler, Belpaire firebox and self-emptying ashpan, Ivatt's 2-6-2T was efficient and low maintenance. Pictured in 1963 at Bournemouth Central, No. 41303 was built under BR at Crewe in 1952. Assigned first to Bricklayers Arms, she spent all of her short twelve-year working life on the Southern Region.

BR Standard Class 4 No. 80081 at Bournemouth Central, 1963. With small modifications, Riddles' class 4 passenger tank was almost a continuation of the former LMS Fairburn 2-6-4T. Riddles, Fairburn, Cox and Ivatt all served under Stanier at the LMS. Their shared heritage is revealed by the family resemblance of many of their designs. The grab crane in the background was used for clearing ash, always a problem at steam sheds.

BR Standard Class 4 2-6-0 No. 76019 stands in a service road near Bournemouth Central shed. Pictured in 1963, the ash and clinker ground-cover is typical for a busy steam depot. Riddles' 2-6-0 class 4 was built at Derby, Doncaster and Horwich between 1952 and 1957, as a lightly modified continuation of Ivatt's LMS class 4. The visually similar 1951 to 1957 Swindon-built 4-6-0 class 4 was developed as a tender version of Riddles' class 4 2-6-4T. Both BR Standard Class 4 tender types were represented on the Southern Region. No. 76019 was built at Horwich in 1953 and spent all of her short twelve-year life operating from Eastleigh and Bournemouth.

Class U No. 31794 near Bournemouth Central shed, pictured in 1963 just weeks before she was withdrawn. Maunsell's 1928 U class consisted of thirty new builds and twenty that were rebuilt from the unsuccessful K class (River class). Identified by a four-window cab front and slightly lower running plates, No. 31794 was one of the K class rebuilds. Known by their crews as 'Rolling Rivers', Maunsell's 2-6-4T K class suffered from instability at speed. No. 800, 'River Cray' overturned near Sevenoaks in 1927. Hard springing, side-tank water surging and poor track alignment contributed to the fatal accident. All twenty of the K class were withdrawn and rebuilt as the 2-6-0 U class. No. 31794, introduced in 1928, was one of seven rebuilt at Eastleigh.

Ash and clinker underfoot, warm oil, steam and sweet smoke. Pictured close to Bournemouth Central shed in 1963, Ivatt 2-6-2T Class 2 No. 41312 stands over the inspection pit, nose to nose with a BR Standard Class 4 2-6-4T. Built at Crewe to a former LMS design, No. 41312 was introduced in 1952, withdrawn in 1967, rescued from scrap and can happily be seen today on the Mid Hants Railway.

Above: Maunsell's last design, class Q were successful and powerful 0-6-0 freight locomotives. No. 30535 stands near Bournemouth Central shed *c.* 1963.

Left: No. 30535, revealing the horizontal cylinders of her Ashford steam reverser. The upper horizontal rod controls valves above the oil cylinder (cataract) on the left and the steam cylinder on the right. Rotating and sliding the control rod pressurises one end of the steam cylinder and allows oil to flow around the cataract pipe circuit. Pressure on the steam piston moves the output shaft until the control valves are closed by the driver to oil-lock the reverser into position. A valve-gear cutoff indicator lever in the cab is driven by the lower rod.

Class M7 No. 30107 makes use of the turntable at Bournemouth Central, *c.* 1963. The smokebox side-mounted Westinghouse air pump reveals this as one of the class members fitted for push-pull working. Built at Nine Elms in 1905, sadly No. 30107 derailed at Raynes Park in 1933 with fatal consequences. Repaired, she continued to complete fifty-nine years of service before withdrawal in 1964.

Bournemouth Central had a busy depot, the turntable was situated at the eastern end, close to the main station buildings. Rebuilt Light Pacific class No. 34022 *Exmoor* at rest *c.* 1963. Built at Brighton in 1946, she was rebuilt in 1957 at Eastleigh. In 1960, she overran signals at St Denys and was derailed by catch-points. Repaired, she continued in service until 1965.

Bournemouth Central shed was located close to the western end of the station. The large locomotive hoist is visible in the centre of the scene. No. 34038 *Lynton*, on the right, was one of the Light Pacific class members to serve until withdrawal in air-smoothed condition. BR Standard Class 5 No. 73020 faces the camera on the left. Pictured in 1963, the site was cleared in 1967 and is now used as a station car park.

Bournemouth shed 1964 with three locomotives posing for the camera. In the foreground, BR Standard Class 4 2-6-4T No. 80146, in the centre Ivatt Class 2 2-6-2T No. 41238 and on the left BR Standard Class 5 4-6-0 No. 73020.

Bournemouth Central shed *c.* 1964. Rebuilt Light Pacific No. 34031 *Torrington* takes centre frame, startling the camera as her safety valves lift. Even in rebuilt form, Bulleid's Pacific classes tended to slip when starting. Heavy use meant that sandboxes needed to be regularly refilled. The steps in the centre of the picture may have been used to help lift containers of sand up to locomotive running plates. BR Standard Class 4 2-6-0 No. 76019 is partly visible on the right.

Introduced in 1950, as one of the last of her Light Pacific class, No. 34105 *Swanage* was built with the sloping cab front that was also retrofitted to earlier class members. Bulleid's original design included streamlined panels, or raves, along the top of the tender sides. These were removed from 1952 to improve rearward visibility and coaling access. Pictured in 1964 by Bournemouth Central shed, and receiving close attention to her steam turbo-generator, she was just months away from withdrawal. *Swanage* was rescued from Barry scrapyard and, as the youngest surviving member of her class, can be seen today on the Mid Hants Railway.

West of Bournemouth Central, the South Western main line runs through picturesque and treelined Meyrick Park. Pictured in 1964, BR Standard Class 5 No. 73002 heads west towards her Weymouth home.

Light Pacific No. 34102 *Lapford* looks spectacular in the afternoon sun as she storms west through Meyrick Park. Even in 1964, her Bournemouth home shed had kept her in immaculate condition.

Meyrick Park was a beautiful location to witness power and grace on the South Western main line. Jarvis' rebuilding programme released the full potential of Bulleid's Merchant Navy design. Pictured in 1964, with safety valves gently blowing, No. 35016 *Elders Fyffes* catches the sun as she storms towards Bournemouth West.

Modified Hall class No. 7918 *Rhose Wood Hall*, pictured in 1964. With a clear exhaust *Rhose Wood Hall* makes good progress away from Bournemouth Central on a Western Region through working. Taking in the views at Meyrick Park, her fireman leans out to pose for the camera.

With one mile to Bournemouth Central, rebuilt Light Pacific class No. 34040 *Crewkerne* heads east through Meyrick Park. In 1961 *Crewkerne* had been involved in a collision with an electric multiple unit at Waterloo. Pictured in 1964, she looks relaxed, steam gently billowing from her safety valves, as she rolls towards Wimbourne Road bridge with an express for fateful Waterloo.

Free steaming, with a soft three-cylinder exhaust beat echoing from the trees, *New Zealand Line* speeds into view. Pictured in 1964, rebuilt Merchant Navy class No. 35021 approaches from Bournemouth West, over Central Drive bridge, with the Up Bournemouth Belle Pullman bound for Waterloo. From 1906 to 1919 the wooden platforms of Meyrick Park Halt stood just beyond the bridge, connected by steps to Meyrick Park Crescent below.

Safety valves lift as the driver shuts the regulator. BR Standard Class 5 No. 73089 *Maid of Astolat* shatters the tranquillity of Meyrick Park with an Up freight in 1964. Built at Derby for the Southern Region, No. 73089 inherited her name from a withdrawn King Arthur class locomotive and carries a large 4,725-gallon BR1B tender. *Maid of Astolat* was named after Elayne of Ascolat, who mythically died of her unrequited love for Sir Lancelot.

Just weeks from her September 1964 withdrawal, battered but still looking magnificent, No. 34091 *Weymouth* glides into view. Completing her fifteen years of service in close to original condition, she continues through Meyrick Park, east towards Bournemouth Central.

Bournemouth West was the terminus for the Somerset & Dorset line, and it also served connections along the South Western main line including Weymouth, Bournemouth Central and Waterloo. Light Pacific No. 34038 *Lynton* waits as BR Standard Class 4 2-6-4T No. 80016 arrives bunker first. Pictured *c.* 1964, and closed in 1965, the site is now under the A338 Wessex Way.

Bournemouth West, *c.* 1964, rebuilt Light Pacific No. 34095 *Brentor* stands in the central relief road with stock ready for a later departure. Light Pacific tenders were smaller than those fitted to the Merchant Navy class, with deeper frames, webbed axle box horn guides, and one instead of two brake shoes per wheel. The raised ledge above the tender side identifies a 5,500-gallon design, the largest fitted to a Light Pacific.

Rebuilt Merchant Navy class No. 35028 *Clan Line* arrives at Bournemouth West, *c.* 1964, with a service from Waterloo. Bournemouth West was connected to the South Western main line via triangular Gas Works Junction to the west of Meyrick Park.

Weymouth station served both Southern and Western Region routes. Boat trains were taken forward to Quay station to connect with Channel Island sailings. BR Standard Class 4 2-6-4T No. 80150 prepares to depart towards Bournemouth West. Pictured just months from her 1965 withdrawal, No. 80150 was interned at Barry scrapyard until 1988, rescued and stored. Now on the Mid Hants Railway, restoration is underway.

Less than a mile north of the station, Weymouth depot was east of the main line and Radipole Park. Closed in 1967, the site is now beneath Milton Close and Prince's Drive. Rebuilt Light Pacific No. 34077 *603 Squadron* with her cousin, rebuilt Merchant Navy, No. 35019 *French Line CGT, c.* 1964, standing on the shed apron. On other pages, *French Line CGT* is pictured in un-rebuilt form at Basingstoke and Salisbury.

Standing in the shadow of Weymouth shed, *c.* 1964, looking out at whispering giants. Rebuilt Light Pacific No. 34077 *603 Squadron*, in the left distance, stands beside the coaling tower. In the foreground, rebuilt Merchant Navy class No, 35019 *French Line CGT* and BR Standard Class 4 2-6-4T No. 80150. On the right, BR Standard Class 5 No. 73017 looks over her shoulder; in the far distance, a Beyer Peacock Hymek waits for her turn.

The former GWR coaling tower, tubs on rails and human toil. Weymouth depot was reallocated from the Western to the Southern Region in 1958. Rebuilt Light Pacific No. 34077 *603 Squadron* has an insatiable appetite. Brake vacuum storage tanks are visible under the tender-top curved cowling, while vacuum brake actuating cylinders sit vertically under the rear buffer beam. In contrast to the relatively clean shed area, piles of ash complete this *c.* 1964 scene.

Above: Rebuilt Merchant Navy class No. 35028 *Clan Line* south of the coaling tower at Weymouth, *c. 1964*.

Left: Rebuilt Merchant Navy class No. 35028 *Clan Line*, close up at Weymouth. Jarvis replaced Bulleid's three sets of chain-driven inside Walschaerts valve gear and steam reverser with a more conventional and reliable design. The outside cylinders were retained but new castings were designed for the inside cylinder. Outside cylinders kept outside admission piston valves whilst the new inside cylinder had inside steam admission. Two outside and one inside set of Walschaerts valve gear were used. Clasp brakes with outside pull rods were retained from the original design. *Clan Line* is preserved and polished today. Pictured *c. 1964*, she wore a thick layer of grease and dirt.

BR Standard Class 4 2-6-0 No. 76065, with a large 4,725-gallon BR1B tender, simmers to the north of Weymouth coaling tower, *c.* 1964. Wagons on the incline through the tower reveal how coal was delivered. Built at Doncaster in 1956 for the Southern Region, No. 76065 spent her entire nine-year working life based at Eastleigh.

Further north of the Weymouth coaling tower, on a road leading to the turntable, Light Pacific No. 34077 *603 Squadron* takes water. The nearby stove stands ready for winter ice. Although No. 34077 was built with a larger 5,500-gallon tender, she's running *c.* 1964 with the smaller 4,500-gallon version fitted originally to earlier class members.

Ivatt Class 2 2-6-2T No. 41293 surrounded by piles of ash beside the incline to the south of Weymouth coaling tower, *c.* 1964. Built at Crewe in 1951 to a former LMS design, No. 41293 spent much of her life based at Eastleigh. She was transferred to Weymouth in 1963 and withdrawn shortly after in 1965. The box visible behind the steps under left side bunker contains batteries for the AWS (Automatic Warning System), standardised from 1957.

Ivatt Class 2 2-6-2T No. 41261 rests at the north end of Weymouth depot, *c.* 1963. For many years, former GWR 1361 saddle tank and 1366 panier tank engines operated the street tramway south from Weymouth station to the quay. From 1963, No. 41261 was one of several of her class to take over this duty. Above the buffer beam, the taller of the collection of four lamps is a of a special design introduced in 1960 for use on the tramway to the quay. The bell on the cab front was used to warn pedestrians on the streets of Weymouth.

Weymouth connected Channel Island ferries to London Waterloo via the South Western main line, and to Paddington via Castle Cary and the Reading to Taunton main line. Pictured *c.* 1964 beside Weymouth shed, and a long way from her St Philip's Marsh Bristol home, Hall No. 4949 *Packwood Hall*, is under repair. The dumbbell-shaped piston valve cover is sitting on the front running plate beside removed access plates.

Close up, though her paint is flaking *c.* 1964, No. 4949 *Packwood Hall* still carries her nameplate with pride. Beautifully cast and polished brass name and number plates gave former GWR locomotives a unique and unmistakeable charm.

Left: Another St Philip's Marsh visitor, Grange No. 6816 *Frankton Grange* temporarily resides at Weymouth shed, *c.* 1963, undergoing serious repairs.

Below: The wheels removed from No. 6816 *Frankton Grange* reveal normally hidden features. Collett's standard bar-frame bogie sits in the foreground. The ATC (Automatic Train Control) sensor with curved metal conduit is visible behind the front crossmember. In the distance, pairs of eccentrics to drive left and right Stephenson valve gear are still mounted on the middle axle.

Light Pacific No. 34002 *Salisbury* is working hard as she climbs the short but steep bank from Exeter St David's into Exeter Central station. Merchant Navy class locomotives often took over at Exeter Central for the run to Waterloo. Pictured in 1963, a wheel tapper stands on the right, long hammer in hand. On the left, happy to disregard the warning sign, a pedestrian prepares to take a short cut.

Pictured in 1963, class W No. 31914 approaches Exeter Central, from the southwest, under Queen Street bridge. Introduced in 1932, the Maunsell-designed 2-6-4T was conceived for London-area short duration freight work. With power and good adhesion, they were ideal for Exeter Central banking and station pilot duties. On the right, Exeter Central B signal box was in service from 1925 to 1970.

Class W No. 31914 prepares to add a restaurant car and coaches to a Waterloo service. Built with three cylinders and three sets of Walschaerts valve gear, class W shared a boiler and standardised components with several of Maunsell's other designs. Bogies and leading wheels were salvaged from the rebuilding of ill-fated K class (River class) 2-6-4T locomotives. Pictured in 1963, the tower on the skyline was part of a Blue Circle cement works served by goods sidings to the north of Exeter Central station.

Released from her train, Light Pacific No. 34002 *Salisbury* has picked up vehicles for her next service. Pausing in a centre road, conveniently near the water crane, *Salisbury* loudly blows off steam as her fireman pulls coal forward. Pictured in 1963, Exeter Central's impressive Queen Street main buildings are visible in the background.

Right: Under plumes of steam and smoke, rebuilt Merchant Navy class No. 35013 *Blue Funnel* energetically arrives at Exeter Central after her 2 hour and 56 minute run from Waterloo. Pictured in 1963, the 'Atlantic Coast Express' divided at Exeter Central with portions running to destinations in Devon and Cornwall. At its busiest summer Saturday peak, the 'Atlantic Coast Express' consisted of up to five separate trains leaving Waterloo in just 40 minutes.

Below: One mile west of Exeter Central, Exmouth Junction is where the line south to Exmouth diverges from the main line to Waterloo. As their Exeter Central (formerly known as Exeter Queen Street) site became too full, in 1887 the LSWR built a new and much larger depot at Exmouth Junction. Looking east from the middle of the depot in 1963, former GWR 5700 Pannier No. 3679 in the distance lines-up with class M7 No. 30125, class Z No. 30951, class 700 No. 30697, class N No. 31409 and, closest to the camera, class 700 No. 30700, all perhaps waiting for their last journey.

Collett 5700 class No. 3679 at Exmouth Junction, 1963. Representing perhaps the most iconic former GWR Pannier, and one of a class of 863, No. 3679 was built at Swindon in 1940 and spent much of her life in South Wales. Transferred to Exmouth Junction in 1959, and withdrawn in March 1963, she awaits her fate.

Pictured in 1963, retired and with front buffers removed, No. 30951 was one of just eight class Z locomotives built at Brighton in 1929 for heavy London-area shunting. No. 30951 had been based at Exmouth Junction since 1959 and used for Exeter Central banking duties. Maunsell's powerful three-cylinder 0-8-0T made use of a boiler design carried over from the earlier C3 class. Outside cylinders, with conventional Walschaerts valve gear, drove the third axle. The steeply inclined inside cylinder drove the second axle. To overcome space and clearance problems, unusually, the inside Walschaerts valve gear combination lever was driven by an additional eccentric.

Class 700 No. 30700 at Exmouth Junction, 1963. After more than sixty-five years of service, No. 30700 was one of the last members of her class of thirty to be withdrawn. Drummond's successful 1897 LSWR 0-6-0 class were upgraded with superheaters and longer smokeboxes from 1919. Drummond had moved to the LSWR from Scotland in 1895. Class 700 were constructed for the LSWR by Dubs & Company at their Queen's Park works near Glasgow.

Built at Eastleigh in 1936, No. 30843 was one of the last S15 batch built by the SR, under Maunsell, as an evolution of Urie's 1920 LSWR design. Maunsell raised the boiler pressure, increased valve travel and fitted larger outside steam pipes. Pictured in 1963, near Exmouth Junction shed, she has straight running plates and a blended cab roof design proposed by James Clayton. Clayton moved from the Midland Railway (MR) to join the LSWR under Maunsell in 1914. Many of the Midland concepts he brought with him were carried forward to other SR designs.

Above: From the centre of Exmouth Junction depot, turning to face northeast opens up a view of the main locomotive shed. Light Pacific class No. 34106 *Lydford* stands in the foreground. Exhaust smoke, and Bulleid's air-smoothed casing, limited visibility. *Lydford* illustrates the sloping cab front fitted post-1947, one of several modifications to improve visibility and control exhaust flow. Former GWR 6400 class Pannier No. 6430 is visible on the right. Pictured in 1963, a recently introduced North British Type 2 'Baby Warship' diesel-hydraulic waits in the shadows.

Left: Exmouth Junction, 1963, Light Pacific No. 34067 *Tangmere* is being prepared. The driver has an oil can ready to top up the feed reservoir. Bulleid's air-smoothed designs could be cleaned by carriage washing equipment. The idea was labour saving but short lived. Locomotives sparkled but washing equipment picked up grime, and carriage windows became oily.

Ivatt Class 2 2-6-2T No. 41272 approaches an inspection pit in front of Exmouth Junction shed, 1963. Ivatt's practical and low maintenance design contrasts with the charm of Collet's 6400 class Pannier No. 6430, and the modernist Bulleid Light Pacific No. 34033 *Chard*. Bulleid's ergonomic design included gauges with night-time ultraviolet lights. Power for electric lighting was delivered by a 24-volt steam turbo-generator mounted under the left cab footplate.

Other Bulleid ergonomic features included steam-powered firebox doors and the use of a steam-powered reverser. While many of Bulleid's concepts worked well, his steam reverser design and oil-bathed chain-driven Walschaerts valve gear needed careful maintenance. Pictured beside Exmouth Junction shed in 1962, in rebuilt form, Light Pacific No. 34032 *Camelford* looks handsome with air-smoothing removed and more conventional Walschaerts valve gear.

With cylinder cocks open, class S15 No. 30841 wheezes slowly backwards. Pictured in 1963, in front of Exmouth Junction shed, No. 30841 is one of the last batches constructed at Eastleigh under Maunsell in 1936. Similar to Urie's N15 King Arthur class, sharing components, but with smaller wheels, S15 locomotives were known as 'Goods Arthurs'. No. 30841 was withdrawn in 1964, rescued from Barry scrapyard in 1972 and ran in preservation until 1994. After a major overhaul she can be seen on the North Yorkshire Moors Railway, running with the frames and the number from her classmate No. 30825.

Rebuilt Merchant Navy class No. 35013 *Blue Funnel* reverses towards the coaling tower at Exmouth Junction. Pictured in 1963, she will run light-engine to Exeter Central and take over the 'Atlantic Coast Express' for the fast run to London Waterloo. *Blue Funnel Line* will work through to the capital, but her crew will change at Salisbury.

BR Standard Class 4 2-6-4T No. 80043 gently reverses beside Exmouth Junction shed. Although Exmouth Junction depot was opened in 1887 by the LSWR, the main concrete and block shed was added by the Southern Railway (SR) in the mid-1920s. At its peak, prior to 1960, Exmouth Junction hosted over 120 locomotives. Pictured in 1963, the depot closed in 1967. The main shed was demolished and replaced in 1979 by a supermarket accessed from Prince Charles Road.

Looking northeast towards the rear of Exmouth Junction shed in 1963, class N No. 31856 reverses towards the turntable. Maunsell assembled a talented and diverse team at the SECR. Harold Holcroft had worked under Churchward at the GWR and James Clayton had worked at the MR. Their influential 1917 class N combined a tapered Belpaire firebox and boiler, outside cylinders, long travel piston valves and a 2-6-0 wheel arrangement inspired by the GWR 4300 class with a cab, smokebox, single crosshead and outside Walschaerts valve gear inspired by Midland practice.

Connected to the Exeter–Salisbury main line at Yeovil Junction, Yeovil Town station opened in 1861 as a LSWR and GWR joint venture. Looking south towards Summer House Hill, reveals a misty scene near the western approach to the station. BR Standard Class 4 4-6-0 No. 75003 stands by on the left as former GWR Small Prairie 4575 class No. 5563 takes water. Pictured, *c.* 1964, Yeovil Town station closed to passengers in 1966. The site is today occupied by a leisure complex.

Class U No. 31632, rests at Yeovil Town, with an open smokebox door. Maunsell's 1928 U class was a direct descendant of his team's influential 1917 class N. Pictured *c.* 1964, No. 31632 is just weeks from withdrawal. In the background, the now demolished stone building on Newton Road once provided overnight lodging for train crews.

Rebuilt Light Pacific No. 34027 *Taw Valley* arrives at Templecombe with a Down train from Salisbury *c.* 1963. Behind the train, the Somerset & Dorset Joint Railway (S&DJR) line from Bath to Bournemouth crosses below the West of England main line. With the 1966 closure of the S&DJR, Templecombe station also closed. Local campaigning succeeded, and the upper station reopened in 1983. Withdrawn in 1964, *Taw Valley* was rescued from scrap and can be seen on the Severn Valley Railway.

Former GWR 5700 class Pannier No. 4631 pauses at Templecombe. Three tank wagons make up the front of the train. Even *c.* 1963, milk travelled by rail. Behind the train, a curve descends to the north-south S&DJR line. Looking northeast, the church of St Mary can be seen in the distance. Parts of the church date from the twelfth century. Templecombe takes its name from the Knights Templar who established Templecombe Preceptory in 1185.

Templecombe depot, looking northeast from Throop road, *c.* 1963. In the distance a southbound train follows the curve to descend from Templecombe upper station to the junction with the S&DJR line. A pilot engine, partly obscured on the right, leads the train down the bank. The train engine, an Ivatt Class 2 2-6-2T is coupled at the rear for the descent. Once the junction has been passed, the train reverses to head south behind the Class 2. Templecombe shed closed in 1966. The site was redeveloped by Plessy Marine Systems and is currently owned by Thalis.

Manoeuvre complete, the Ivatt Class 2 2-6-2T continues her journey south. Pictured *c.* 1963, Templecombe depot hosts a former GWR 2251 class in the right foreground, nose to tail with a former LMS Fowler class 4F, in the distance, another 2251 class stands beyond a mineral wagon.

Templecombe depot, standing beside the S&DJR line, looking southeast, *c.* 1963. Throop road, the vantage point for earlier pictures, runs past the lattice fence in the distance and over a bridge out-of-frame on the right. 5700 class Pannier No. 4691 rests in front of 2251 class No. 3216. Both are examples of Collett's design work, and were built at Swindon for the GWR.

The S&DJR was set up as a joint venture of the LSWR and MR. Pictured at Templecombe depot *c.* 1963, S&DJR 2-8-0 7F No. 53810 pauses by the turntable. The S&DJR 2-8-0 was built from 1914 by the MR under Henry Fowler. Much of the design work was carried out at Derby by James Clayton, who would later join Maunsell at the SECR. Well suited to the steeply graded lines of the S&DJR, the 7F 2-8-0 was ideal for freight and, when needed, heavy summer passenger services.

Atmospheric Bath Green Park, the northern terminus for the S&DJR, *c.* 1963. Passengers board as Fowler 4F No. 44422 becomes eager to depart. Shared by the LMS and SR, then part of the BR Southern then Western Region, Bath Green Park often hosted through-workings to the North West. On summer Saturdays, the station was busy with trains reversing to continue their journey. Closed to passengers in 1966 the arched roof fortunately remains. No. 44422 has been preserved on the Churnet Valley Railway.

Looking southeast towards Bath Green Park S&DJR shed, *c.* 1963. Green Park station was located a short distance behind the shed, on the other side of the River Avon. Fowler 4F 0-6-0 No. 44422 lurks inside the wooden shed on the far left. In the foreground, her 4F classmate No. 44102 on the left prepares beside BR Standard Class 4 4-6-0 No. 75073. On the right, BR Standard Class 5 No. 73049 stands below the coaling stage. This fascinating site has been redeveloped as a retail park on appropriately named Stanier Road.

Salisbury, *c.* 1962. Yeovil Town-based class U No. 31614 arrives from the west with a local working. Situated at the intersection of the former LSWR West of England main line from Waterloo to Exeter, and the former GWR Wessex main line from Bristol to Southampton, Salisbury was a busy and historically interesting station.

Light Pacific No. 34015 *Exmouth* arrives at Salisbury, *c.* 1962, with a local service from Exeter. *Exmouth* served until withdrawal in air-smoothed condition. Bulleid's powerful Light Pacific class were capable of performing well with heavy West Country summer loads. At other times, they could often be seen hauling local services with just a few coaches.

Vivid green, illuminated by summer afternoon sun, rebuilt Light Pacific No. 34052 *Lord Dowding* runs into Salisbury from the West. Pictured in the early 1960s, Salisbury-based *Lord Dowding* was rebuilt from her original air-smoothed condition in 1958. Salisbury West signal box is visible near the rear of the train. Using equipment from the British Pneumatic Railway Signal Co., the LSWR installed a low pressure compressed air signalling system in 1902. Pneumatic signals operated at Salisbury until 1981.

Rebuilt Light Pacific No. 34052 *Lord Dowding* at Salisbury in the early 1960s. Bulleid's Light Pacific class were named after West Country locations, and after squadrons and heroes of the Battle of Britain. Many had iconic oval shields fashioned in vitreous enamel with a cast brass surround. Air Chief Marshal Dowding led RAF Fighter Command during the Battle of Britain.

Class M7 No. 30033 operating as station pilot at the west end of Salisbury, *c.* 1962. The LSWR and the GWR originally operated separate adjoining stations at Salisbury. From 1932, GWR trains shared the former LSWR station. The ex-GWR 'Salisbury C' lever frame signal box, visible in the distance, operated from 1901 to 1973.

Crew change at Salisbury, *c.* 1963. Tired, and in drizzling rain, the Waterloo crew are hard at work. Perhaps looking forward to a cup of tea in the mess room, the driver guides the water bag while the fireman pulls coal forward. In the foreground, the relief crew get ready to take over. With her new crew on board, rebuilt Merchant Navy class No. 35024 *East Asiatic Company* will continue to Exeter.

Rain or shine, every day, every hour, with similar choreography, a repeating performance. The London fireman pulls coal forward, while his replacement replenishes tender water. Unaware, in warm compartments, passengers enjoy a moment of quiet at Salisbury. Pictured *c.* 1963, wearing a thick coat of soot, rebuilt Merchant Navy class No. 35006 *Peninsular & Oriental S.N. Co.* is heading west towards Exeter. Rescued from scrap, restored and usually gleaming, No. 35006 can often be seen today on the Gloucestershire Warwickshire Railway.

Rebuilt Merchant Navy class No. 35006 *Peninsular & Oriental S.N. Co.*, Salisbury, *c.* 1963. Bulleid's Merchant Navy class were named after shipping lines involved in the Battle of the Atlantic or operating from the Southern port of Southampton. Tubular sandbox fillers stand below the nameplate. The flexible cable of the speedometer can be seen in the lower right.

Light Pacific class No. 34054 *Lord Beaverbrook* prepares to head west from Salisbury. No. 34054 illustrates the air-smoothed condition typical *c.* 1962. As an early class member, No. 34054 was built with short smoke deflectors and a flat cab front. Standard length deflectors and a sloping cab front were retrofitted in the late 1940s. Tender-top raves and fairings in front of the cylinders were removed in the early 1950s. An AWS battery was fitted above the front buffer beam from 1959.

Eastleigh-based BR Standard Class 4 2-6-0 No. 76060 arrives at Salisbury, *c.* 1963. Services from Southampton, Portsmouth, Bournemouth, Brighton and other southern locations arrived at Salisbury from the east. Trains heading north departed to the west, travelling on former GWR lines, parallel to the LSWR main line. Three miles west of Salisbury, near Wilton, the Wessex main line diverges to the north for services to Bristol and South Wales.

Wessex main line services often changed locomotive at Salisbury. Perhaps picking up a service from Portsmouth, Modified Hall class No. 6973 *Bricklehampton Hall* prepares to head back to her Cardiff home. Pictured *c.* 1964, the vans beyond the wall on the left are on lines leading to the goods depot on the site of the former GWR station. The goods depot closed in 1991, the site is currently used by Salisbury Traincare Depot.

Schools class V No. 30936 *Cranleigh* with a Down train at Salisbury. Maunsell's three-cylinder class V were the most powerful 4-4-0 design in Europe. Built at Eastleigh, and introduced in 1930, the class of forty were named after English public schools. A round-top firebox, and a 4-4-0 wheel arrangement, allowed operation on lines with a restricted loading gauge and short turntables. Pictured *c.* 1959, while based at Bricklayers Arms, *Cranleigh* was withdrawn in 1962.

Simmering gently in mid-gear, class U No. 31632 has arrived at Salisbury. Pictured *c.* 1962 with a Down train, No. 31632 was built at Ashford in 1931 as one of the final batch of ten. To the north, beyond the wall, the former GWR broad gauge station was built as a terminus in 1856. In 1859, the LSWR opened their station on the current site. From 1860 to 1902 a covered footbridge, a connecting shed and new platforms were added by the LSWR to close the gap between the two stations.

Salisbury *c.* 1959, class U No. 31791 arrives from the west. No. 31791 was rebuilt from the earlier and unsuccessful River class at Eastleigh in 1928. Salisbury goods depot stood beyond the wall, on the site of the former GWR terminus, north of the current station. In 1874 the GWR converted to standard gauge, and by 1859, lines connected the two stations.

Former GWR Castle class, No. 5073 *Blenheim*, rolls in from the east to take over an inter-regional express from the South Coast. Pictured, *c.* 1962, *Blenheim* will take the service forward from Salisbury, along the Wessex main line, and towards her Cardiff home. No. 5073 was renamed in 1941, from *Cranbrook Castle* to *Blenheim*, as a tribute to the Bristol Blenheim light bomber.

Salisbury, *c.* 1952, Merchant Navy class No. 35019 *French Line CGT* arrives with a train from Waterloo. Just three years after the *c.* 1949 picture taken at Basingstoke, No. 35019 is seen with her Southern Railway stripes and smokebox roundel replaced by standard BR lined green. Rebuilt in 1959, *French Line CGT* is pictured on other pages at Weymouth in her later form.

Pictured, *c.* 1962, rebuilt Light Pacific No. 34010 *Sidmouth* runs into Salisbury with a Down train. *Sidmouth* has been preserved and is currently undergoing restoration. On the right, a Thomas Cook poster suggests that travellers should 'Ask the man at Cooks…he knows!'

With a pick balanced precariously on the tender roof, two firemen work together to pull coal forward and break up larger lumps. With her new crew on board, rebuilt Light Pacific No. 34062 *17 Squadron* will continue east towards Waterloo. The large water tank above the heads of the crew was part of the former GWR station. Pictured *c.* 1963, it still stands today at the east end of Salisbury station.

The Up working of the 'Atlantic Coast Express', with rebuilt Merchant Navy class No. 35013 *Blue Funnel* in charge. Coal is pulled forward, water taken on and a new crew takes over. Pictured *c.* 1962, with safety valves blowing vigorously, *Blue Funnel* is eager to begin the non-stop eighty-three-mile run to Waterloo. The GWR water tower is visible on the right. In the distance, goods vans mark the location of the former GWR station.

Rebuilt Merchant Navy class locomotives were fitted with additional sand pipes for the leading and middle driving wheels. Even in rebuilt form, traction remained a weakness of Bulleid's Pacific designs. Despite the skill of her driver, rebuilt Merchant Navy 35013 *Blue Funnel* slips as she pulls away from Salisbury, *c.* 1962. Steam billows as her driver releases sand to help grip.

Light Pacific No. 34005 *Barnstaple* leaves Salisbury for Waterloo. As an early class member, No. 34005 was built with a flat cab front and short smoke deflectors. Exhaust smoke, and Bulleid's air-smoothed casing, limited visibility. Pictured *c.* 1952, a sloping cab front has been retrofitted together with experimental extra-long smoke deflectors. Tender-top raves and a fairing in front of the cylinders are both still in place. Panels above the front buffer beam illustrate the configuration before the addition of AWS. A short-lived slide bar dust cover, fitted from 1948, is also visible above the crosshead. The footbridge behind the train went to the former GWR station, part of which is visible on the right.

Salisbury, *c.* 1952, looking east from the footbridge. Class L12 4-4-0 No. 30415 coasts towards the station. Introduced by Drummond for the LSWR in 1904, the L12 class were affectionately known as 'Bulldogs'. No. 30415 was withdrawn months later in 1953. Infamously, it was a speeding class L12 that caused the fatal 1906 Salisbury rail crash. Behind the train on the left, Salisbury East signal box controlled pneumatic signals. On the far left, the rear of advertising hoardings above Fisherton Street can be seen.

Class S15 No. 30834 approaches Salisbury from the east with a Down freight train, *c.* 1962. Identified by a blended all-steel cab roof, No. 30834 was built in 1927 as a Maunsell evolution of Urie's original 1920 S15 design. While the majority of the S15 fleet ran with eight-wheel tenders, No. 30834 is running with a six-wheel tender to allow operation with shorter turntables. Girders beside the train mark the location of the Fisherton Street bridge.

Class U No. 31636 heads east from Salisbury. A former GWR coach at the head of the train suggests a through working from the Western Region. Pictured *c.* 1952, No. 31636 still carries early British Railways lettering on her tender. Behind the train, the pitched roof of the water tank and the connecting overbridge are visible. On the right the glass gable of Brunel's original GWR train shed can be seen.

King Arthur class N15 No. 30450 *Sir Kay* runs light-engine to the east of Salisbury station, *c.* 1952. No. 30450 is one of the batch built under Maunsell in 1925 as a continuation of Urie's design. The two-cylinder King Arthur class and Maunsell's larger four-cylinder Lord Nelson class had been the mainstay of the Southern Railway's express passenger fleet during the 1930s.

BR Standard Class 4 2-6-0 No. 76007 heads east from Salisbury on a particularly wet day. Behind the train, the pitched roof of the GWR water tank is still visible. Pictured *c.* 1963. The overbridge and the train shed roof have been removed.

Arriving at Salisbury on a Waterloo to Exeter service, *c.* 1962. On the right, rebuilt Merchant Navy class No. 35010 *Blue Star* departs for Waterloo. The colour of the sleepers on the right reveal that on the Up departure line, sand was frequently deployed. Signal posts in the foreground have been freshly repainted. The vertical cylinder of the pneumatic actuator can be seen on the left of the lattice signal post.

Andover Junction, *c.* 1964, rebuilt Merchant Navy class No. 35003 *Royal Mail* arrives from the southwest. Seventeen miles from Salisbury, Andover Junction connected the West of England main line with the former Midland & South Western Junction Railway line from Swindon to Southampton. The curved roof behind the chimneys may house the top of a goods lift.

Rebuilt Merchant Navy class No. 35003 *Royal Mail* leaves Andover Junction, bound for Waterloo. *Royal Mail* was built in 1941 and rebuilt in 1959. As an early class member, she ran for much of her life with 5,000-gallon tender. Pictured *c.* 1964, she's paired with a rebodied 5,250-gallon design, identified by a continuous tender upper edge.

Winnersh Halt in the late 1950s. Schools class V No. 30911 *Dover* heads southeast from Reading on the North Downs line towards Guildford and Redhill. The route through Winnersh is shared with the Reading to Waterloo line, upgraded with 660-volt third-rail electrification in 1939. Former GWR and SR classes could often be seen at Winnersh. The Forest School is visible on the right.

Redhill, looking northwest, *c.* 1960. Class U No. 31631 prepares to take the North Downs route for Guildford and Reading. An ex-LNER van is coupled next to the tender. The Brighton main line from London had been electrified though Redhill since 1933. South of Redhill, the North Downs line branches to the west and the line for Tonbridge branches to the east.

Tunbridge Wells West, *c.* 1960, class H 0-4-4T No. 31533 pauses with a train for Tonbridge. Class H were introduced by Wainwright for the SECR in 1904. Sixty-four of the original class of sixty-six were in service after nationalisation. Between 1949 and 1960, forty-five were fitted for compressed air push-pull operation. The Westinghouse air pump is visible on the side of the smokebox. The cylindrical vertical regulator-actuator can be seen on the front of the side tank.

Tunbridge Wells West, looking east towards Montacute Road bridge, *c.* 1960. Class H No. 31533 propels the train in push mode towards Tunbridge Wells Central and Tonbridge. Push-pull services connected Tunbridge Wells West to destinations including Three Bridges and Oxted. The site of Tunbridge Wells West station has been redeveloped into a supermarket. Lines to the west of the station are now part of the Spa Valley Railway.

Oxted, *c.* 1960, looking south. BR Standard Class 4 2-6-4T No. 80017 runs in with a service from Tunbridge Wells West to London Victoria. On the left, class H No. 31543 prepares to leave with a push-pull service for Tunbridge Wells West.

Eridge, looking northwest, *c.* 1960. BR Standard Class 4 2-6-4T No. 80018 arrives with a service from Tunbridge Wells West to Polegate and Eastbourne. Eridge station remains open, but sadly the Cuckoo line south from Eridge to Polegate closed in 1965. The route north to Tunbridge Wells West closed in 1985 and is now operated by the Spa Valley Railway.

Class K 2-6-0 No. 32348 is ready to depart from Polegate Junction. Designed by Billinton for the LBSCR, the seventeen K class locomotives were built at Brighton between 1913 and 1921. The majority of railway companies in Britain used vacuum brakes, but from 1877 the LBSCR became one of the first to use air brakes. The Westinghouse air brake pump can be seen on No. 32348 near the cab front. Closed in 1986, Polegate Junction stood at the intersection of lines north to Eridge, west to Lewes, east to Hastings and south to Eastbourne. Looking east, *c.* 1960, gas lamps are still in use.

Eastbourne, *c.* 1960, class U1 2-6-0 No. 31892 waits for the right away. Class U1 were a slightly more powerful three-cylinder evolution of the successful two-cylinder U class. The prototype U1 was rebuilt from a three-cylinder K1 version of the earlier unsuccessful River class 2-6-4T. Although Maunsell and Holcroft experimented with Gresley-inspired conjugated valve gear for the middle cylinder, the U1 class of twenty built from 1928 to 1931 used three sets of Walschaerts valve gear.

Newhaven Town *c.* 1961, looking southwest from Station Approach (close to the path of the current B2109 Drove Road). Pedestrians wait patiently as class E4 0-6-2T No. 32509 gently creaks past. Billinton's 1897 E4 class of seventy-five were built for the LBSCR at Brighton for branch line mixed traffic duties. Popularly known as 'Radials' because of the radial axle boxes of the trailing wheels, the majority of the class had long lives. No. 32509 was withdrawn in 1962 after sixty-one years of service.

Wadebridge to Ilfracombe via Halwill, Bude and Barnstaple

Wadebridge, 254 miles from Waterloo, close to Padstow, the Southern Railway's most western outpost. Looking northeast towards the river Camel, *c.* 1963, former GWR 1366 class No. 1367 gently propels vans beside the station. No. 1367 and two of her classmates were moved from Weymouth to Wadebridge in 1962 to replace ageing Beattie well tank locomotives on the Wenford Bridge branch.

Class 1366 No. 1367 continues her shunting movement beside Wadebridge shed and water tower, *c.* 1963. Introduced in 1934, Collett's 1366 class of six were built at Swindon as a Pannier tank evolution of Churchward's earlier 1361 class Saddle tanks. Unusually for a small GWR design, both used outside cylinders with inside Allan straight-link valve gear. The majority of the design work on the 1361 class was undertaken by Harold Holcroft. Holcroft later moved to the SECR to become an influential member of Maunsell's team.

Wadebridge, *c.* 1963, Light Pacific class No. 34015 *Exmouth* arrives with a train from Exeter to Padstow. On the left, lifting-legs stood in front of the locomotive shed. On the right, a 'fire devil' brazier stands beside the water crane, ready to deal with winter ice. Although Wadebridge station was closed to passengers in 1967, the station buildings and canopy can still be seen on Southern Way.

Left: Halwill Junction, looking southwest, *c.* 1963, class N No. 31874 has arrived from the Okehampton direction. Lines north from Halwill diverged, curving southwest to Wadebridge and Padstow, branching west to Bude and northeast to Torrington and Barnstaple Junction. Halwill Junction closed in 1966. A housing development with the hauntingly named Beeching Close stands on the site today. Built at Ashford in 1925, No. 31874 was withdrawn in 1964, restored and can be seen on the Swanage Railway.

Below: Bude, *c.* 1963, BR Standard Class 4 2-6-4T No. 80064 prepares to leave with a local service for Halwill. Bude was, for many years, served by a segment of the 'Atlantic Coast Express' from Waterloo. Split at Halwill, portions would head west to Bude and southwest to Padstow. The station closed in 1966 and has been redeveloped with housing on Bulleid Way. Withdrawn in 1965, No. 80064 was rescued and is on display at the Bluebell Railway.

Barnstaple Junction was at the confluence of the former LSWR main line from Exeter to Ilfracombe with the route north from Halwill and Torrington. With the closure of the former GWR Victoria Road station in 1960, Barnstaple Junction also became the starting point for services to Taunton. Pictured *c.* 1963, former GWR 4300 class No. 7304 prepares to depart for Taunton.

Class 2 2-6-2T No. 41297 rests close to Barnstaple Junction *c.* 1963. A locomotive hoist can be seen on the right. No. 41297 was built at Crewe in 1951 as a continuation of Ivatt's 1946 design for the LMS. Versatile and successful, eventually 130 were in service.

Barnstaple Junction, *c.* 1963 looking north towards the station and goods yard. With deafening safety valves, Class N No. 31848 looks shabby but keen, while her driver conscientiously works with his oil can. At its First World War peak, the Woolwich Royal Arsenal had a skilled workforce of 80,000. As part of post-war recovery efforts, and an aborted railway nationalisation plan, the Ministry of Supply issued a contract for the Arsenal to make 100 kits of parts for Maunsell's successful class N. Built in 1925, No. 31848 was one of a batch of fifty, affectionately known as 'Woolworths', built at Ashford from Royal Arsenal kits.

Barnstaple Junction shed, looking north, a Bulleid Light Pacific catches the sun, a Maunsell class N rests in shadow. The roof of the wooden locomotive shed appears to have remained intact until at least 1960. Pictured *c.* 1963, the shed is in terrible condition.

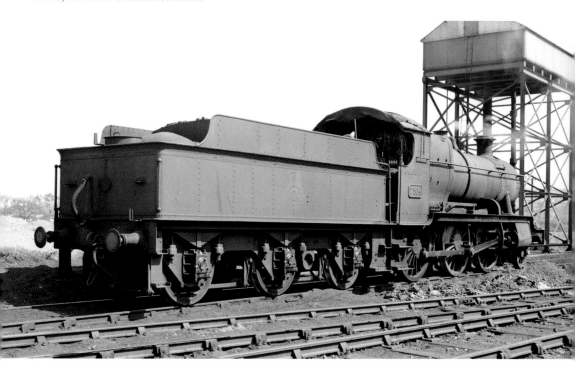

Barnstaple Junction, behind the shed, looking southeast, *c.* 1963. Former GWR 4300 class No. 7304 simmers gently beside the water tower. As Maunsell built his team at the SECR he recruited Harold Holcroft from the GWR. Holcroft had worked under Churchward to design the successful 4300 class. Using Holcroft's GWR experience, Maunsell's class N was designed with a 2-6-0 wheel arrangement, long-travel piston valves, and a tapered Belpaire firebox and boiler similar to those of the 4300 class.

Ilfracombe, Light Pacific No. 34106 *Lydford*, more than 100 tons moved by two men. A short distance south of the station, Ilfracombe's unusual lattice girder turntable was squeezed into land carved from the hillside. Chatting on a pleasant day, *c.* 1963, I was happy to accept the driver's offer of a footplate ride back to the station.

Light Pacific No. 34106 *Lydford*, turned and ready to reverse to Ilfracombe station, *c.* 1963. Hidden under the air-smoothed casing, occasionally leaking or stuck, boiler feedwater clacks could be difficult to reach. On the footplate, a tale was shared of a cab visit from Mr Bulleid. Hearing the drivers experience, Bulleid indignantly replied, 'driver, my clacks do not stick or leak!' As Chief Mechanical Engineer, he was undoubtedly a proud parent.

Opened by the LSWR in 1891, from 1923 Eastleigh Works became the principal engineering site for the Southern Railway. Today, many of the buildings remain in railway use. At, or close to withdrawal in 1964, class U No. 31804 stands near the running shed at Eastleigh. Designed by Maunsell just ten years after the end of the First World War, it's not surprising that class U were nicknamed 'U-boats'. Identified by low running plates and a four-window cab front, No. 31804 was built at Brighton in 1928 as one of a batch rebuilt from unsuccessful SECR 2-6-4T River class locomotives.

As a descendant of Maunsell's class N, class U can trace many of their design elements back to Churchward and the former GWR 4300 class. Pictured in 1964, close to withdrawal at Eastleigh Works, class U No. 31628 is one of the first batch to be newly built. No. 31628 was built at Ashford in 1929 and can be identified by higher running plates and a modified cab profile. In BR service, the class U fleet were fitted with BR Standard Class 4 chimneys. As cylinders wore and needed to be replaced, many also received BR Standard Class 4 cylinders. An AWS battery box is visible between the running plate and the sloping manual reverser rod.

Class S15, No. 30512, recently withdrawn at Eastleigh, 1964. In contrast to the SECR heritage of Maunsell's U class, Urie's S15 was developed for the LSWR. While the SECR had adopted the tapered Belpaire firebox and boiler shape of the GWR, the LSWR made use of a parallel boiler with a round-top firebox. Evolved from the H15 King Arthur class but with smaller wheels, class S15 were affectionately known as 'Goods Arthurs'. As one of the first batch, No. 30512 was built at Eastleigh in 1921.

Pictured close to the running shed at Eastleigh in 1964, class S15 No. 30824 is still in service. With the 1923 grouping of the LSWR and SECR as two of the SR constituents, Urie retired and Maunsell became the SR Chief Mechanical Engineer. As a member of the second S15 batch, No. 30824 was built at Eastleigh in 1927, and reveals Maunsell's design influence. Valve travel was improved, boiler pressure increased. More visible design changes include straight running plates and a Midland-inspired all-steel cab.

One of a class designed by Stroudley for the LBSCR and affectionately known as 'Terriers', class A1X No. 32650, originally named *Whitechapel*, was built at Brighton in 1876. After a career of nearly eighty-seven years with duties including London commuter work, a secondment to the Isle of Wight, shunting at Lancing Works, experimentation with oil firing and a jaunt on the Hayling Island branch, she found herself in a line of withdrawn locomotives pictured at Eastleigh in 1964. Unlike the LSWR and the SECR, the LBSCR used air brakes. A Westinghouse air brake pump is fitted to the cab side of No. 32650. Fortunately, No. 32650 was rescued and can be seen at the Spa Valley Railway. Sadly, class M7 No. 30107 was not as fortunate.

Built in 1903 at Nine Elms for the LSWR, class M7 No. 30133 managed a still-impressive sixty-one years of service. From 1912, thirty-one members of Drummond's M7 class were fitted with a cable and pulley system for push-pull working. Unreliable, and perhaps unsafe, the system was replaced from 1930 by a compressed air system that had been successfully used by the LBSCR. Pictured at Eastleigh in 1964, No. 30133 is fitted with a Westinghouse pump for compressed air push-pull operation. Early M7 class members were fitted with a lever reverser, No. 30133 was fitted with a steam-powered reverser. Later class members were fitted with boiler feed pumps and feed water heating, No. 30133 was fitted with more conventional injectors.

Maunsell completed the design work on his Q class shortly before he retired in 1937. The class were built from 1938 at Eastleigh after Bulleid had taken over as the SR Chief Mechanical Engineer. Pictured in 1964, class Q No. 30548 has returned to Eastleigh for her last months of service. The row of bolts below the smokebox shows the inclination of the two inside cylinders. Piston valve spindle end-covers can be seen below the smokebox door. Although some members of the fleet were fitted with BR Standard Class 4 chimneys, No. 30548, like the majority of her class is running with a Lemaître multi-jet blast pipe retrofitted by Bulleid to improve steaming.

Although projecting a strikingly different aesthetic, Bulleid's Q1 owes much to its Maunsell Q class ancestor. Both use an 0-6-0 wheel arrangement, similar sized inside cylinders, piston valves driven by rocking levers and conventional Stephenson valve gear. Both have a similar wheelbase and driving wheel diameter. The Q1 steam reverser, visible above the centre driving wheel, closely follows the design of the Q class. Despite their many mechanical similarities, Bulleid was able to design his Q1 with a larger and higher pressure boiler to deliver 15 per cent more tractive effort, making Q1 the most powerful 0-6-0 class in Europe. Bulleid used a Lemaître multi-jet blast pipe, Firth Brown wheels and a tender that followed design patterns already established for his pacific classes. Pictured at Eastleigh in 1964, class Q1 No. 33033 is sadly just weeks away from withdrawal.

Rebuilt Light Pacific No. 34005 *Barnstaple*, recently overhauled beside the running shed at Eastleigh, 1964. During 1957, *Barnstaple* was the first of Bulleid's Light Pacific class to be rebuilt. Without her air-smoothed casing, the profile of Bulleid's excellent boiler can be more clearly seen. Feed water clacks are visible behind the chimney. Unusually, Bulleid's design had both clacks on the right-hand side of the boiler. Feed pipes run from the two injectors below the cab footplate. Controls are conveniently positioned for the fireman working on the right-hand side of the footplate. *Barnstaple* is pictured on other pages in air-smooth condition at Salisbury.

As the world's only all-electric Pullman train, the 'Brighton Belle' was unique. Three 5-BEL five-car sets were built by Metro-Cammell for the Southern Railway to run on their newly electrified third-rail London Victoria to Brighton route. Introduced in 1933 and named 'Brighton Belle' from 1934, marquetry, wood panelling and Art Deco styling created a luxurious passenger experience. Fourteen of the original fifteen vehicles survive. The 5-BEL Trust are caring for six vehicles as part of a project to bring the 'Brighton Belle' back to life. Seven vehicles are in the custody of Belmond British Pullman who run the Venice Simplon Orient Express and one is in private hands. Pictured in 1973, shortly after their 1972 withdrawal, No. S291S, S292S, S293S, S287S, S285S and S286S, perhaps not yet sure of their fate, stand near Mistley in Suffolk.

Ryde Pier Head on the Isle of Wight, 1964. Class O2 No. W14 *Fishbourne* waits on the left as O2 No. W28 *Ashey* departs for Ryde Esplanade. Opened in 1814, the world's oldest pleasure pier was enlarged with a horse-drawn tramway in 1864 and a railway in 1880. Frequent ferry services connected the Isle of Wight railway to Portsmouth Harbour.

Ryde Pier Head station and the line to St John's Road was opened in 1880 as a LSWR and LBSCR joint venture. A new pier carrying the railway line was constructed parallel to the existing pleasure and tramway piers. Pictured in 1964, class 02 No. W30 *Shorwell* has been released from her train at Ryde Pier Head.

Ryde St John's Road, 1964, class O2 No. W29 *Alverstone* arrives on the Isle of Wight Railway route from the south. Originally named Ryde station, St John's Road opened as a terminus in 1864. The line beyond St John's Road bridge in the distance leads to Ryde Pier Head.

From 1923, the five railway companies operating on the Isle of Wight were grouped into the SR. Suburban electrification released steam locomotives on the mainland. The SR moved former LSWR O2 class locomotives to the Isle of Wight. Pictured in 1964, class 02 No. W30 *Shorwell* arrives at St John's Road with a train from Ryde Pier Head.

South of St John's Road, the Isle of Wight Central line branched west towards Havenstreet. Fireman and signalman cleverly perform a double token exchange as class O2 No. W26 *Whitwell* arrives at Havenstreet from the east with a train for Newport and Cowes. Pictured in 1964, Havenstreet closed in 1966 but since 1971 has been operated as a heritage line by the Isle of Wight Steam Railway.

Pictured in 1964, class 02 No. W14 *Fishbourne* takes water at Newport before continuing north to Cowes. When the SR moved class O2 locomotives to the island, they were renumbered in sequence, or with the number of the withdrawn locomotive they replaced. Named after Isle of Wight towns and villages, at their peak twenty-three class O2 operated on the island.

Right: Ventnor on the south coast was the terminus for the Isle of Wight Railway from St John's Road. Pictured in 1964, class O2 No. W30 *Shorwell* pauses at the southern end of the station to take water as she runs round her train. In the distance, coal merchants operated from former quarry chambers on the left.

Below: Class O2 No. W30 *Shorwell* taking water near the north of Ventnor station in 1964. Introduced by Adams for the LSWR in 1889, class O2 were developed for London commuter services. No. W30 moved to the island in 1926. For Isle of Wight operation, each locomotive was fitted with air brakes and a Westinghouse pump. Rear bunkers were extended from 1932 to improve range.

Ventnor signal box stands guard beneath a dramatic chalk backdrop. Pictured in 1964, class O2 No. W17 *Seaview* enthusiastically heads into the 1,312-yard tunnel under St Boniface Down with a train for Ryde Pier Head.

Class O2 No. W30 *Shorwell* catches the sun on a bright summer day in 1964. Just two years later, in its centenary year, Ventnor station closed. Today, the site is used for an industrial park. The once beautifully picturesque tunnel and chalk face remain.